All THINGS MANATEES For Kids

FILLED WITH PLENTY OF FACTS, PHOTOS, AND FUN TO LEARN ALL ABOUT SEA COWS

ANIMAL READS

WWW.ANIMALREADS.COM

THIS BOOK BELONGS TO...

_____

_____

WWW.ANIMALREADS.COM

WHAT'S FLOATING IN HERE?

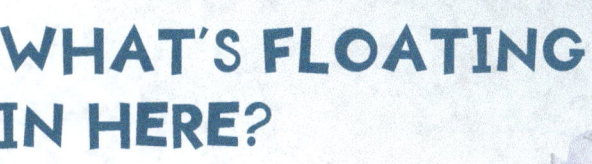

Welcome to the Exciting World of Sea Cows! 1

Manatees 101: 5
   What ARE These Adorable Sea Cows?

Manatee Features: 13
   From Flippers to Whiskers

Meet the Manatee Family! 23

Manatee Homes: 35
   Where Do They Live?

What's On The Manatee Menu?............. 43

Growing Up Manatee: 51
   From Calf to Giant

Fun Facts About Manatees................... 59

Hooray! You're a Manatee Expert! 69

Thank You! 73

WELCOME TO THE EXCITING WORLD OF SEA COWS!

Have you ever heard of a sea cow? No, we are not talking about a cow that swims in the sea, but you are on the right track!

Meet the manatee (pronounced man-uh-tee), a large, gentle, and downright adorable marine animal that's earned this fun nickname. Manatees look like giant teddy bears with flippers instead of arms and legs!

We're so happy you want to learn about these amazing animals. In this book, we'll dive into their world! We'll discover where they live, what yummy foods they eat, and learn cool facts to make you a true manatee expert. Did you know that manatees are related to elephants? Yes—those huge animals that live on land! We'll explore this and other surprising facts about these special creatures.

Manatees are gentle and curious animals. They spend their days floating through warm, shallow waters, eating plants. They're calm like cows, but don't say "*moo.*" Instead, they make chirps and squeaks that will make you smile!

Grab your life jacket because we're about to start an exciting adventure with these friendly water giants.

Let's go say hello to the manatees!

WATER YOU WAITING FOR?

MANATEES 101:
WHAT ARE THESE ADORABLE SEA COWS?

Manatees are amazing **marine mammals** that love to swim! Marine mammals are animals that live in water but breathe air, just like we do. Manatees mostly live in oceans and explore magical places like lagoons and coastal wetlands. *But guess what?* These gentle giants can also be found in freshwater rivers and **estuaries**. An estuary is a special place where rivers meet the sea!

Manatees share the water with other sea creatures like playful dolphins, giant whales, and cute sea turtles. Like these animals, manatees smoothly glide through the water, making oceans and rivers their happy home!

WHAT ARE MAMMALS?

Mammals are special animals that share certain features. First, they are warm-blooded, which means their bodies stay warm even when it's cold outside. Whether it's a hot sunny day or a chilly cloudy one, a manatee keeps its body temperature just right.

Another cool fact is that all mammals have fur or hair at some point in their lives, even if it's just a little bit! Manatees have tiny, bristly hairs on their bodies that help them feel things around them. And here's something amazing: mammals feed their babies with milk! So whether they're huge like elephants or tiny like mice, all mammals **are warm-blooded**, have some kind of **hair**, and **drink milk** from their mothers when they're babies.

Can you name some other mammals? How about dogs, cats, and horses? Even big animals like elephants and lions are mammals! And guess what? **We humans are mammals too!** Just like manatees, we have hair, keep our bodies warm, and drink milk as babies.

Yup, even us! We're all mammals!

Within the mammal group, manatees belong to a special family called **Sirenia** (say: sigh-REE-nee-uh). Think of Sirenia as a big family where everyone has things in common, like paddle-shaped flippers and slow, gentle swimming. This family also includes the manatee's cousins, who are called **dugongs** (say: DOO-gongs)!

I'm a dugong! My tail looks different from a manatee's—it's more like a dolphin's! And I only live in the ocean!

Manatees also belong to a smaller group called **Trichechus** (say: try-KEK-us). The name "Trichechus" comes from Greek words that refer to the manatee's special whiskers! All members of the Trichechus club have rounded tails (*unlike their dugong cousins who have fluked tails like dolphins*), the same kind of teeth, and they all live in warm waters.

These funny names are all part of the manatee's **scientific classification.**

WHAT IS A SCIENTIFIC CLASSIFICATION?

Scientific classification uses special names to explain how animals are sorted into groups. It's like organizing your toys into different boxes: you might have a box for cars, one for dolls, and another for building blocks. This helps you find your toys quickly and keeps everything neat. Scientists sort animals in a similar way to learn more about them and how they're related!

ANIMAL READS

Fun Fact:

Manatees can grow as long as a small car (about 13 feet or 4 meters) but are gentle and peaceful. They have flippers shaped like paddles, which they use to steer and move slowly through the water. Their slow swimming is actually a smart trick that helps them save energy!

Now that we're beginning to learn about manatees, let's dive deeper and see what makes them so special.

WHEN IN DOUBT, JUST FLOAT IT OUT!

MANATEE FEATURES:
FROM FLIPPERS TO WHISKERS

Manatees have extraordinary features that help them thrive in their watery homes! From their great big flippers to their wrinkly skin, everything of the manatee is tailor-made for life underwater.

PADDLE-SHAPED FLIPPERS

Have you ever seen a canoe paddle? Manatees have flippers that look just like those paddles! Their flippers are wide and flat, helping them move smoothly through the water. Just like you would use paddles to steer a boat, manatees use their flippers to turn left, right, or even spin in playful circles!

These unique flippers also help manatees "walk" along the bottom of rivers and oceans while looking for yummy plants to eat. Imagine being a manatee, moving your flippers gently, and finding tasty underwater snacks—wouldn't that be fun?

Flippers? Paddle-shaped. Tail? Paddle-shaped. I'm built for gliding through the water!

WRINKLY SKIN

Manatees have thick, wrinkly skin that often gets covered with tiny green plants called algae (say: AL-jee). These tiny plants like to grow on manatees, sometimes giving them a greenish color! Their skin is tough and leathery, working like armor to protect them from sharp rocks and other things underwater.

Those funny wrinkles aren't just for looks—they actually help manatees stay cool in warm waters.

ALL THINGS MANATEES　15

The wrinkles create more skin surface, which helps their body temperature stay comfortable. Pretty clever, right?

> My wrinkles don't mean I'm old—they're just part of my look!

WHISKERED SNOUTS

What's with those whiskers, you ask?

Manatees have special whiskers on their noses that can feel the tiniest movements in water! These whiskers, called **vibrissae** (say: vye-BRISS-ee), help

With whiskers like these, maybe they should call me a 'sea cat' instead of a sea cow!

them find food underwater. When a manatee swims near some seagrass, its whiskers can tell which plants are the tastiest, making mealtime easy! Imagine having a magic nose that could feel things in water and tell you which foods are the yummiest.

If we had noses *like that, they'd probably lead us straight to all the pizza!*

ALL THINGS MANATEES 17

Wait... did someone just say pizza?!

CHUBBY BODIES

Manatees are famous for their big, round bodies—*but why are they so chubby?* The main reason is their thick layer of blubber. Blubber is a special type of fat that helps marine mammals like manatees in many ways.

First, blubber acts like a cozy blanket! Even though manatees live in warm, shallow waters, it can still get chilly sometimes, especially in winter. Their blubber keeps them nice and warm, trapping their body heat and keeping the cold out.

Second, blubber is like a snack stash! Manatees munch on many tasty plants, storing the extra energy in the blubber. Sometimes, when food is hard to find, they can use the energy stored in their blubber to keep them going until they discover more delicious treats.

Finally, blubber helps manatees float effortlessly in water. This special fat acts like a built-in life jacket! Thanks to their blubber, manatees can drift along gracefully without sinking. How cool is that?

QUIRKY PERSONALITIES

Manatees aren't just interesting to look at—they also have sweet and curious personalities! People often call them the "gentle giants" of the sea, and they truly deserve this nickname.

While manatees usually swim alone, you might sometimes see them in small groups, especially when a mother is with her baby, called a calf. Baby manatees stay with their mothers for up to two years, learning important skills to grow strong and healthy.

These curious animals love exploring their underwater homes and sometimes even swim up to say hello to people! Can you imagine swimming and suddenly meeting a friendly manatee? Even though they're big (*about as long as a car*), manatees are gentle and move slowly, making them the true peaceful giants of the water world.

JUST A FLOATING POTATO!

MEET THE MANATEE FAMILY!

Alright, little explorers! Now that you know what a manatee is, it's time to meet the whole family! Like you have brothers, sisters, and cousins, manatees have different family members, too—in the animal world, they're called **species** (say: SPEE-sees).

There are about 60,000 manatees in the world, divided into three different species: the West Indian Manatee (also called the Florida Manatee), the Amazonian Manatee, and the African Manatee. All three species are considered **vulnerable**, which means their natural homes are slowly being damaged. Luckily, many conservation groups are working hard to protect these amazing animals. *Conservation means taking care of animals and the places they live so they'll be around for a long time.*

Are you as excited as we are to meet them? Let's get to know these sensational water buddies!

> I'm a West Indian Manatee! You can find me all over Florida's warm waters!

WEST INDIAN MANATEE (FLORIDA MANATEE)

These friendly hulks are the largest members of the manatee family. Imagine a creature as long as a small car gliding peacefully through the water—that's the West Indian Manatee! They love warm, shallow waters where they can munch on tasty seagrass all day. If you ever visit sunny Florida—especially places like Miami or the Florida Keys—keep your eyes open! You might spot one of these gentle giants floating by.

ALL THINGS MANATEES   25

West Indian manatees are truly impressive in size. They can grow to be between 9 and 13 feet long (about 2.7 to 4 meters)—that's about **the length of two or three kids lying head-to-toe**! They're about 4 to 5 feet tall (1 to 1.5 meters), just a bit taller than a door handle, and weigh between 800 and 1,200 pounds (360 to 540 kilograms), as heavy as a grand piano!

The West Indian Manatee lives in the coastal waters and rivers of the southeastern United States,

the Caribbean, and even parts of South America. These animals have no natural **predators** (*animals that hunt them*), so they spend their days peacefully exploring and eating their favorite plants. *Why hurry when no one's chasing you?* Watching a manatee swim by is like spotting a bit of magic in the water—gentle, curious, and always calm. So, if you ever get the chance, watch these majestic creatures as they go about their underwater adventures!

    ALL THINGS MANATEES   27

I'm an Amazonian Manatee—smaller, but still mighty!

AMAZONIAN MANATEE

Even though they're **the smallest type of manatee**, Amazonian Manatees are full of surprises. Unlike their relatives who like salty water, these little blobs of wonder live only in freshwater, making their home in the famous **Amazon River.** The Amazon is the second-longest river in the world, crossing eight countries in South America.

This is the Amazon River! It may be the second longest in the world, but it's the largest—carrying more water than the next seven biggest rivers combined!

Do you know?

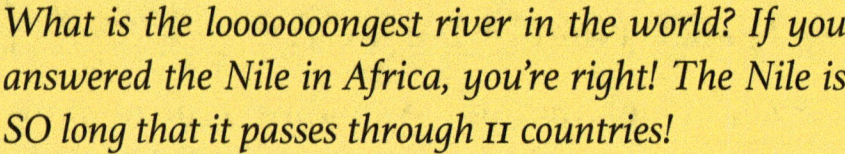

What is the looooooongest river in the world? If you answered the Nile in Africa, you're right! The Nile is SO long that it passes through 11 countries!

With their smooth, dark skin, the Amazonian manatees blend perfectly into the river's murky waters, becoming experts at hide-and-seek. They're naturally shy and enjoy hiding among water plants in the Amazon Basin, where they feel safe and cozy.

ALL THINGS MANATEES   29

Amazonian Manatees may be small compared to other manatees, but they're still pretty huge. They grow from 7 to 9 feet long (about 2 to 2.7 meters), roughly **the length of one and a half to two kids lying down**! They stand about 3 to 4 feet tall (0.9 to 1.2 meters)—around **the height of a kindergartener**—and can weigh between 700 and 1,000 pounds (320 to 450 kilograms), **similar to a small horse**. Their size and gentle nature make them perfect for life in the lush, winding waterways of the Amazon.

These manatees have amazing hearing that helps them detect sounds underwater. This super hearing is important because the Amazon water is often

murky, making it hard to see very far. If you're lucky to explore the Amazon Basin, keep your eyes open—you just might get a glimpse of one of these gentle freshwater giants hiding among the plants!

I'm an African Manatee—rare, mysterious, and totally cool!

AFRICAN MANATEE

Let's give a big wave to the African Manatee! These friendly sea cows are adventurers who can live in both freshwater rivers and salty ocean waters. African Manatees can be in rivers, exploring

estuaries (*where rivers meet the sea*), or swimming along the spectacular coasts of West Africa. With their curious and adventurous spirit, they're always on the move, discovering new places and enjoying different water homes.

African Manatees grow to an impressive length of around 9 to 11 feet (2.7 to 3.3 meters)—about **as long as an adult bicycle from wheel to wheel!** They stand about 3.5 to 4.5 feet tall (1.1 to 1.4 meters), **close to the height of a dining room table,** and weigh between 800 and 1,200 pounds (360 to

540 kilograms), as heavy as a **grand piano or large motorcycle**. Their strong build and powerful tails help them navigate through different types of water.

What makes African Manatees special is their ability to live in both fresh and saltwater, making them the most **adaptable** members of the manatee family. This **adaptability** (say: a-dapt-a-BIL-i-tee) means they can live in many different areas. If you ever visit West Africa, keep looking—you might be lucky enough to see one of these gentle giants gracefully gliding through the waves!

Now you know about the three species of manatees! Each one has its own unique traits and favorite places to call home, but they all share a gentle nature that makes them lovable. Now, you're ready to learn more about their incredible homes and behaviors!

WHY DID THE MANATEE CROSS THE ROAD?

To SEA the other tide!

MANATEE HOMES:
WHERE DO THEY LIVE?

Now that we've learned about the fantastic traits and the different species of manatees, it's time to explore their special homes *or what scientists call* **habitats**! Manatees have some pretty cool places to live, and each species has its favorite hangout spots. But before we dive into the details, let's talk about what we mean by "**habitat.**"

WHAT IS A HABITAT?

A habitat is the natural home of animals and plants. It's a special place where animals find everything they need to survive: **food to eat, water to drink, and safe places to rest and raise their babies.**

Think about your own habitat—*your house and neighborhood.* That's where you have your family, your bed, your kitchen, and places to play. Manatees also need their own special habitats where they can live, grow, and raise their babies.

NATURAL HABITATS

Manatees love to hang out in warm coastal waters, rivers, and estuaries. They love living in these places because they are filled with fantastic plants and super cozy places to rest. Manatees especially like shallow, slow-moving waters where lots of seagrass grows.

Imagine living in an underwater, edible garden full of your favorite treats—that's exactly the kind of habitat manatees love! These waters also keep manatees warm and safe from big, hungry predators.

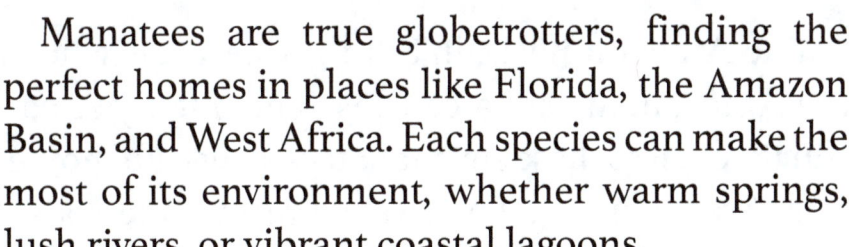

FAVORITE HOMES AROUND THE WORLD

Manatees are true globetrotters, finding the perfect homes in places like Florida, the Amazon Basin, and West Africa. Each species can make the most of its environment, whether warm springs, lush rivers, or vibrant coastal lagoons.

Florida and the Caribbean is a perfect habitat for the West Indian Manatee. Florida's warm coastal waters and rivers are a manatee paradise. If you visit Miami or other coastal areas, ask the adults with you if you can go on an amazing boat tour to meet the wonderful Florida Manatee!

The Amazon Basin in South America is where the Amazonian Manatee lives. The mighty Amazon River gives these shy manatees a peaceful home full of tasty plants. The river's murky waters also help hide them from danger, making it the perfect spot for these quiet manatees to eat and rest.

ALL THINGS MANATEES

West Africa's warm, shallow waters are where African Manatees live. What makes their habitat special is that they can live in both freshwater rivers and salty coastal areas. From rushing rivers to calm bays along the coast, West Africa offers many different places for these adaptable manatees to explore.

ANIMAL READS

Each manatee species has found the perfect home that matches its special needs and habits. These habitats provide everything manatees need: plenty of food, warm water, and safe places to raise their babies.

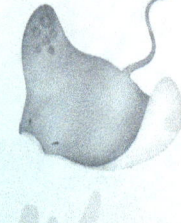

Some call it seagrass, manatees call it dinner!

WHAT'S ON THE MANATEE MENU?

Manatees are what are called **herbivores**, meaning they only love munching on plants like cows enjoy their grass. But instead of a grassy field, manatees have their very own salad bar right in the water! Their meals consist of various water plants, including seagrasses, algae, and other tasty underwater vegetation.

Seagrasses are the manatee's main food. These plants are full of nutrients, grow in shallow, sunny waters, and provide a healthy meal for these gentle giants. Manatees also love **water hyacinths**, which are floating plants usually growing in freshwater rivers and lakes. Another of the manatee's favorite treats is **hydrilla**, a thick, nutrient-packed plant that grows in mats beneath the water's surface. Manatees also love munching on **algae**, which grows on rocks and the bottoms of rivers and oceans.

Mmm... I love me some seagrass!

Here's the coolest part: **manatees use their lips to scrape the algae off rocks and the seafloor!**

Manatees have a unique way of eating that helps them enjoy their plant-based diet. They use their **strong, flexible upper lips** like fingers to grab and pull the plants into their mouths. These special lips can move in many directions, helping manatees pick exactly which plants they want to eat. Once they have a tasty treat, they chew it with their **molars** – those are the flat teeth at the back of their mouths. These teeth keep growing throughout their lives to replace ones worn down from all

their munching. And trust us, they do a LOT of munching!

Manatees **spend about 8 hours every day eating**! With their slow metabolism and large appetites, manatees certainly know how to savor their meals.

MANATEE PREDATORS

Even though manatees are gentle giants, they do have a few **natural predators** to watch out for. *But what exactly is a predator?* Predators are animals that hunt and eat other animals, often using

special skills like sharp teeth, claws, or speed to catch their meals. While manatees may seem invincible, a few creatures can pose a threat, especially to younger ones.

SHARKS

The larger species of sharks, like bull sharks, might see young manatees as a snack. However, don't worry too much! Manatees usually hang out in shallow waters, where these sharks don't often

roam. This makes shark attacks on adult manatees rare, although young calves are more vulnerable.

ALLIGATORS

In freshwater areas, alligators are another potential threat to young manatees. Luckily, adult manatees are so big that alligators usually leave them alone. Still, baby manatees need to be cautious when swimming in places where alligators live.

HUMANS

Sadly, one of the biggest threats to manatees actually comes from humans. Boats are especially dangerous because manatees swim slowly and often stay near the water's surface, making it easy for them to get hit by boats. This is why many areas where manatees live have special speed limits for boats.

Pollution in the water, on land, and in the air also harms manatees by destroying their natural homes. This is perhaps the biggest challenge manatees face today. That's why many conservation groups work hard to protect these animals and the places they live.

Despite these dangers, manatees have developed smart ways to stay safe. Their calm, slow-moving nature helps them avoid getting the attention of predators. They prefer shallow waters, which makes it harder for larger predators to reach them. Thanks to these peaceful habits and some help from humans who care about protecting them, manatees continue to thrive in the wild.

CAUTION

MANATEE AREA

SLOW AND STEADY WINS THE SEAWEED!

GROWING UP MANATEE:
FROM CALF TO GIANT

Manatees go through many life stages, each one an exciting adventure! From taking their first breath to exploring the underwater world on their own, manatees have an amazing journey through life. Let's dive into the remarkable story of how these gentle giants grow up.

BIRTH AND EARLY LIFE

Manatee calves, or baby manatees, are born underwater, making their entrance into the world truly special! When they're born, they're already about 4 feet long and weigh around 60 pounds—that's about the size of a child's bicycle. Right after being born, these babies must quickly swim to the water's surface to take their very first breath of air!

Even though they're babies, manatee calves are strong swimmers from their first day of life. For their first two years, they stay close to their mothers,

Double trouble? Yup, we're twins! Manatee twins are super rare!

drink milk (*called nursing*), and learn important survival skills. During this time, they begin to explore their watery home and learn how to find tasty water plants to eat.

A mother manatee's milk is very rich and helps her calf grow quickly. Baby manatees can start eating plants when they're just a few weeks old, but they continue drinking their mother's milk for up to two years.

ALL THINGS MANATEES 53

Milk break time! This West Indian manatee calf is sticking close to mom.

GROWING UP

As they get older, manatees enter their "teenage" years, which scientists call adolescence (say: ad-oh-LESS-ence). They are between 2 and 5 years old and start exploring more on their own, although they still depend on their mothers for help—a lot like you might rely on grown-ups in your life.

This time is very important for manatees to practice swimming, eating plants, and learning to find their way around their habitat. Young manatees

discover more food sources and learn the skills they'll need to survive on their own, like how to dodge pesky predators and find safe napping spots.

During this time, young manatees grow quickly. They develop stronger swimming skills and start to look more like adult manatees.

ADULT LIFE

By the time manatees are 4 to 5 years old, they're fully grown into powerful swimmers who can find plenty of food. Adult manatees can live for up to 40 years in the wild, though they may live even

longer—up to 60 years—in places like aquariums and wildlife parks where they receive regular care and food.

Adult manatees spend their days swimming, eating, and sometimes socializing with other manatees. When it's time to have babies, male manatees gather around a female, and she chooses which one will be her mate. After mating, the female manatee carries her baby inside her body for about a year (*this is called pregnancy*), which is one of the longest pregnancies of any marine mammal. This long growing time ensures the baby is strong enough when it's born.

Female manatees usually have one calf every 2-5 years throughout their adult life. They're very caring mothers who teach their babies everything they need to know about being a manatee.

This amazing cycle of life continues, helping manatees survive for generations!

WHAT'S A MANATEE'S GO-TO HAIRSTYLE?

A MANE-a-tee!

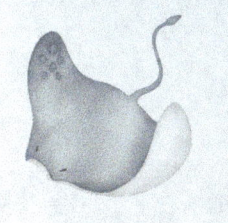

FUN FACTS ABOUT MANATEES

We don't know about you, but we can't get enough of these incredible beasts! They are fascinating and definitely among the most unique creatures on earth.

C'mon, let's review what we have learned so far and find out more!

MANATEES AND ELEPHANTS ARE LONG-LOST COUSINS!

Guess what? Manatees are related to elephants! That's right! Even though manatees swim in the water and elephants walk on land, they share a common ancestor. That means they had the same great-great-great (*many "greats"*) grandparent animal millions of years ago.

Looking closer, you might see that both manatees and elephants have thick, wrinkly skin and bristle-like hairs. How cool is that? Funnily enough, their

I'm a hyrax—believe it or not, I'm family with manatees and elephants!

closest living buddies are tiny creatures called **hyraxes**, which look like fluffy guinea pigs but are actually more closely related to manatees and elephants than to rodents.

MANATEES ARE GREAT AT HOLDING THEIR BREATH UNDERWATER

Like all mammals, manatees breathe air through their lungs. When they're swimming or eating, they need to come up for air every 3 to 5 minutes. But here's something impressive: these gentle giants can hold their breath for up to 20 minutes when they're resting!

ALL THINGS MANATEES 61

Imagine holding your breath for that long—you'd need super-sized lungs! And that's exactly what manatees have. Their big lungs help them stay underwater for a long time, perfect for taking a relaxing nap without having to hurry to the surface.

MANATEES TAKE UNDERWATER NAPS

You might wonder how manatees sleep if they need to breathe air. Instead of one long sleep like we have at night, manatees take short naps that last just a few minutes at a time, all day and night.

When napping, they either float just below the water's surface or rest on the bottom of shallow

areas. *The coolest part?* Even when they're asleep, their bodies automatically rise to the surface when it's time to breathe! It's like they have a built-in alarm clock that works even during sleep.

Manatees get about 10 to 12 hours of sleep every day—similar to humans—but they break it up into many little naps throughout the day and night. This way, they stay well-rested while always being ready to breathe when needed.

MANATEES ARE CHATTIER THAN YOU THINK

Even though manatees look quiet, they actually "talk" to each other! They make sounds like squeaks, chirps, and whistles that other manatees can hear underwater.

These sounds help manatees stay in touch with each other and are especially important when mother manatees need to call their babies. If you're ever near manatees in the water, listen carefully—you might hear them chatting with each other!

MANATEES ARE VEGETARIAN

Manatees are **herbivores**, which means they only eat plants. They spend most of their days munching on seagrass and other tasty water plants, just like cows graze on grass in a field.

Because plant food gives less energy than meat, manatees need to eat a lot—up to 10 to 15% of their

body weight every day! That would be like a 60-pound child eating 9 pounds of vegetables daily. Good thing manatees have big round bellies to hold all that food!

MANATEES ARE SLOW BUT IMPRESSIVE EXPLORERS

They might swim slowly, but manatees can travel incredible distances! Some manatees migrate (move seasonally) to warmer waters during winter months, swimming hundreds of miles to find cozy spots with plenty of food.

It's like going on a long road trip, except you're swimming the whole way instead of riding in a car! Florida manatees often travel from the coast to inland springs when the ocean gets too cold, making a journey that can be over 100 miles long.

TOO COOL FOR FAST SCHOOL!

HOORAY! YOU'RE A MANATEE EXPERT!

Wow! Look how much you've learned! We've explored the wonderful world of manatees diving into their fascinating lives, delicious diets, cozy homes, and so much more. **You've unlocked the secrets of these gentle giants, and now you're a true sea cow expert.** What an incredible journey it has been!

Take a moment to celebrate everything you've learned about these remarkable creatures. Manatees are so much more than just cute animals—they're vital parts of our ecosystems, and now you know just how amazing they truly are.

But don't keep your newfound knowledge to yourself—share it with your friends and family! Tell them about manatees, and impress them with all the fun facts you've discovered. Whether you're chatting about their seagrass salads or their incredible underwater adventures, you'll be the life of the party with your manatee expertise.

As you keep learning about our world, remember that there are countless amazing animals waiting to be discovered. From the deepest oceans to the highest treetops, and even in your own backyard, fascinating creatures are everywhere! Each bit of knowledge brings us closer to being better friends with the animals that share our planet.

Thank you for being such an enthusiastic and curious reader! We hope you continue to discover and appreciate the incredible animals around us.

Until our next adventure, happy exploring!

MANATEES ALWAYS SEA-ZE THE DAY!

THANK YOU!

Thank you for reading this book and for allowing us to share our love for manatees with you!

If you've enjoyed this book, please let us know by leaving a rating and a brief review wherever you made your purchase! This helps us spread the word to other readers!

Thank you for your time, and have an awesome day!

For more information, please visit:
www.animalreads.com

WHAT'S A MANATEE'S FAVORITE DANCE MOVE?

The Sea Cow Shuffle!

© Copyright 2025 — All rights reserved Admore Publishing

ISBN: 978-3-96772-188-1

ISBN: 978-3-96772-189-8

ISBN: 978-3-96772-190-4

Animal Reads at www.animalreads.com

The content contained within this book may not be reproduced, duplicated or transmitted without direct written permission from the author or the publisher.

Under no circumstances will any blame or legal responsibility be held against the publisher, or author, for any damages, reparation, or monetary loss due to the information contained within this book. Either directly or indirectly.

Published by Admore Publishing: Gotenstraße, Berlin, Germany

www.admorepublishing.com

www.ingramcontent.com/pod-product-compliance
Lightning Source LLC
LaVergne TN
LVHW021340080526
838202LV00004B/249